D0459126

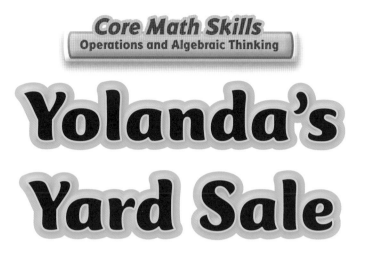

Core Math Skills
Operations and Algebraic Thinking

Yolanda's Yard Sale

Add and Subtract Within 20

Malcolm Hoban

PowerKiDS press™

NEW YORK

Published in 2014 by The Rosen Publishing Group, Inc.
29 East 21st Street, New York, NY 10010

Book Design: Mickey Harmon

Photo Credits: Cover, pp. 5, 22 Lifesize/Thinkstock.com; p. 7 (background) Palette7/Shutterstock.com; pp. 7, 11, 21 (doll) Artmim/Shutterstock.com; pp. 7, 21 (blocks) Iakov Filimonov/Shutterstock.com; pp. 7, 21 (ball) Elena Schweitzer/ Shutterstock.com; pp. 9, 11, 19 (box) Vitaly Korovin/Shutterstock.com; pp. 7, 9, 21 (bear) grekoff/Shutterstock.com; pp. 7, 9, 21 (white bear) thanapun/Shutterstock.com; pp. 7, 11, 21 (yo-yo) Mike Flippo/Shutterstock.com; pp. 11, 21 (baseball) Dan Thornberg/Shutterstock.com; p. 13 maraga/Shutterstock.com; pp. 15, 21 (wood grain) Reinhold Leitner/ Shutterstock.com; p. 17 (table) Lightspring/Shutterstock.com; p. 17 (lemonade) Layland Masuda/Shutterstock.com.

Library of Congress Cataloging-in-Publication Data

Hoban, Malcolm.
Yolanda's yard sale: add and subtract within 20 / Malcolm Hoban.
  p. cm. – (Core math skills. Operations and algebraic thinking)
Includes index.
ISBN 978-1-4777-2064-6 (pbk.)
ISBN 978-1-4777-2065-3 (6-pack)
ISBN 978-1-4777-2211-4 (library binding)
1. Addition—Juvenile literature. 2. Subtraction—Juvenile literature. 3. Garage sales—Juvenile literature. I. Title.
QA115.H63 2014
513.2'1—dc23

Manufactured in the United States of America

CPSIA Compliance Information: Batch #CS13RC: For further information contact Rosen Publishing, New York, New York at 1-800-237-9932.

Word Count: 334

Contents

Making Money   4

Things to Sell   6

Sending Invitations   12

At the Yard Sale   18

Time to Party!   22

Glossary   23

Index   24

Making Money

Yolanda wanted to throw a pizza party, but she had no money in her piggy bank. She could make money by selling her old toys. She decided to have a yard sale.

Things to Sell

Yolanda looked around her room for old toys. She found 7 toys under her bed and 8 toys in her toy box. Then, she found 4 toys on her **desk**. Yolanda found 19 toys to sell!

bed   toy box   desk

7 + 8 + 4 = 19

Yolanda used to **collect** teddy bears. She found 2 brown bears and 2 black bears. Then, she found 3 white bears. She had 7 bears to sell.

$$2 + 2 + 3 = 7$$

$$4 + 3 = 7$$

Yolanda used to collect other things, too. She had 4 yo-yos and 4 baseballs. Then she found 1 doll. There were 9 things altogether.

$$4 + 4 + 1 = 9$$

$$8 + 1 = 9$$

Sending Invitations

Yolanda made **invitations** for her yard sale and took one to each house on her street. There were 8 white houses and 2 red houses. There were 7 blue houses, too. She had to make 17 invitations altogether.

8 + 2 + 7 = 17

10 + 7 = 17

Yolanda also made 14 **fliers** to give away. She made the fliers on colorful paper. First, she gave away 4 green fliers. Then, she gave away 5 pink fliers. There were 5 yellow fliers left to give away.

$$14 - 4 - 5 = 5$$

$$10 - 5 = 5$$

Yolanda made lemonade for her **customers**. She made 12 cups and set them on her table. Her brother drank 2. Then her sister drank 1. They drank 3 altogether. Yolanda had 9 left!

$$12 - 2 - 1 = 9$$
$$10 - 1 = 9$$

At the Yard Sale

Yolanda had 5 bears in a box. Then, she sold 2 to her friend Melinda. She had 3 bears left. She wanted the box to look full, so she put 2 more bears in the box. There were 5 bears again!

5 - 2 = 3

3 + 2 = 5

Yolanda's yard sale was a hit! She started out with 19 toys. By noon, she sold 9 toys. Then, she sold 2 more. In all, she sold 11 toys. How many toys did she have left to sell?

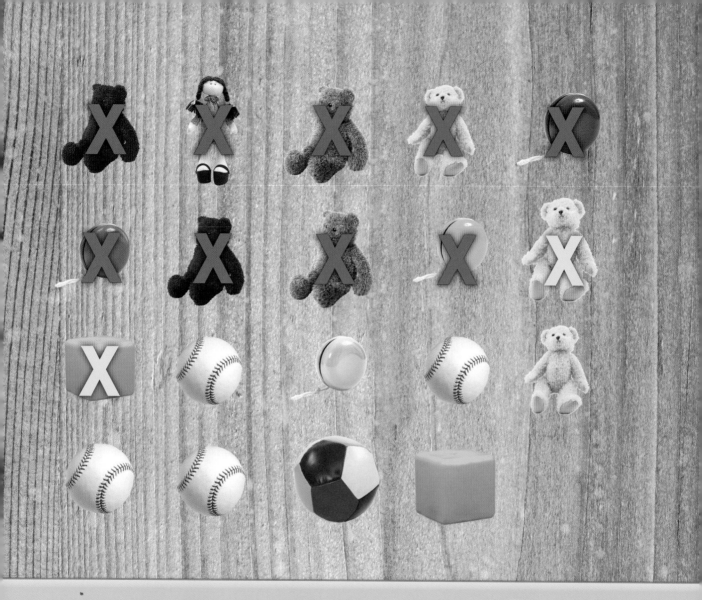

$$19 - 9 - 2 = ?$$
$$10 - 2 = ?$$

21

$17 - $15 = ?

Time to Party!

Yolanda made 17 dollars at her yard sale. Now, she could have her party! A pizza costs 15 dollars. How much money did she have left over?

Glossary

collect (kuh-LEHKT) To gather together.

customer (KUHS-tuh-muhr) Someone who buys
    something from a business.

desk (DEHSK) A table used for reading, writing,
    or drawing.

flier (FLY-uhr) A paper telling people about something.

invitation (ihn-vuh-TAY-shun) A card asking someone to
    come to a place or event.

Index

baseballs, 10

bears, 8, 18

customers, 16

doll, 10

dollars, 22

fliers, 14

house(s), 12

invitations, 12

lemonade, 16

party, 4, 22

pizza, 4, 22

toys, 4, 6, 20

yo-yos, 10

Due to the changing nature of Internet links, The Rosen Publishing Group, Inc., has developed an online list of websites related to the subject of this book. This site is updated regularly. Please use this link to access the list: www.powerkidslinks.com/cms/oat/yys